BEING W

CW00408507

BEING WITH

A Course Exploring Christian Faith and Life

Participants' Companion

Sally Hitchiner

CANTERBURY
PRESS

Norwich

© Sally Hitchiner 2022

First published in 2022 by the Canterbury Press Norwich
Editorial office
3rd Floor, Invicta House
108–114 Golden Lane
London EC1Y 0TG, UK

www.canterburypress.co.uk

Canterbury Press is an imprint of Hymns Ancient & Modern Ltd
(a registered charity)

Hymns Ancient & Modern® is a registered trademark of
Hymns Ancient & Modern Ltd
13A Hellesdon Park Road, Norwich,
Norfolk NR6 5DR, UK

British Library Cataloguing in Publication data
A catalogue record for this book is available
from the British Library

ISBN 978 1-78622-442-2

Typeset by Regent Typesetting
Printed and bound in Great Britain by
CPI Group (UK) Ltd

Contents

Introduction

Welcome to the Being With course!

The Being With course was written by Revd Dr Sam Wells and me, Revd Sally Hitchiner, as we worked together at St Martin-in-the-Fields church. We wanted to find a way to help people who found themselves on the edges of our church to explore the Christian faith afresh. The heart of what we believe is that God's methods are never different from what God wants to communicate, so we wanted the course to *feel* like our message as well as speaking it. There are lots of ways to discover the facts about what Christians believe through books or websites, but there is only so much you can learn through facts. So we created this course to be an immersive experience of learning how to be with ourselves, with others and the world around us, and learning how to be with God.

Spoiler Alert

The course isn't a Bible study or a series of arguments to try to convince you that God exists. We're not anxious to fix you. We start with the belief that you already have a wealth of experiences of truth, beauty and goodness that will help you, in discussion with others, to find God, just from your normal experiences of life.

We also start with the idea that God's greatest desire is to be with us in Jesus. That's the reason the world was created. It's the reason

Jesus died: he wasn't going to abandon us even if it meant he was caught up in something that killed him. This being with God is the ultimate destination of humanity. Christianity isn't fundamentally about sin. It's not about being good enough to pass the test to get to the good place when you die. It's certainly not about excluding people. God wants to be with us. God wants to be with you and every other human being who has ever lived, and God wants us to be with God. That's it. That's the litmus test for working out what is authentic Christianity and what isn't.

The course is about helping you to discover yourself and God and to learn to be conscious of God being with us in the world. It's also about learning to be with others. The course gathers people from a wide variety of life experiences. We are aware that the normal ways of interacting often reinforce hierarchies and expectations of who someone is. Because we ask participants to step into a different way of interacting with each other from the one you'd have in a social or work context, we hope to disrupt this and create more opportunity for people to be truly themselves and experience a more authentic version of the others in their group.

How to use this guide

This companion guide is intended to walk with you through the course. There's no need for any prior religious knowledge or language: just what you have learnt in your life so far. Respond to a personal or general invitation: you may be asked for some contact information but no one should chase you if you decide it's not for you; and then just show up at the first meeting, onsite or online. I'll explain our methods as we go, as your course hosts will do. It's more about getting into a way of interacting than about doing things in a certain way, but I've added a little introductory explanation for the first few weeks to familiarize you with the key components of the course. Either you can either read each week's content before you do your session in the group, or you can read it afterwards if you missed something. The course is about the experience of being in a group rather than the information you'll learn, so the focus should be on the group. Some people feel more able to engage with a group if they know what is likely to happen; others find it distracting. If you're the type of person who feels more comfortable knowing what's coming throughout the entire course then do read the introductions to the welcome and wonderings in advance.

The ten-week course of 90-minute onsite or online video-conference group meetings of six to 14 people has two leaders, one called the host and the other called the storyteller. Each week follows the same four-part pattern:

Welcome – This is an invitation to be with yourself as you start the session and to share something of who you are right here and now with the group.

Wonderings – The centre of the course is not information, but an invitation to be with others and wonder about significant areas of life together. We ask people to receive what is shared without comment or competition but as a gift, with a simple 'Thank you'.

Talk – Our own experiences are then brought into dialogue with thinking about the being-with themes from around the world and throughout history.

Reflection – This is an opportunity to ease back into the way we interact in normal life, in dialogue and discussion. You can raise thoughts, objections and questions about what you've heard, and reflect together with other participants about what it might mean in your life.

Who are we?

As you're putting your future in our hands, I should tell you a little about who we are. As well as being vicar of St Martin-in-the-Fields, Sam is a globally recognized academic theologian who specializes in theology that is immersed in real life. His writing about being with is celebrated by archbishops and professors in the most prestigious universities in the world. My contribution is 20 years of experience of reimagining the interface between church and society in the national media, and building Christian communities in universities, churches and online with people who find churches inaccessible. In any of those contexts, there is little space for faith that isn't serious enough to hold real life. I want to know God in real life. I'm not interested in helping people to reduce who they are as if that will make it easier to find real faith. This course hopes to help you be more who you are, engage with more about your fellow humanity and the world around us and discover more about who God really is. We cannot really know someone from a distance. We can only really know ourselves, others or God by risking sharing ourselves and by being open to friendship. That's the heart of our method: inviting you to explore relationship.

This participants' guide is written with thanks to those who trusted us enough to come on the early courses as we figured things out. It takes guts to put yourself forward to explore faith when you haven't explored it before. Perhaps it takes even more courage to put yourself forward to be part of a guided group exploring faith when you have had bad experiences of church. In the world-weary days of the Covid-19 pandemic, these people have led Sam and me to a fresh discovery of our faith as they invited us to discover Jesus afresh through their eyes. Is there a better gift? We wouldn't be here without their honesty, hope and kindness. You know who you are.

Week One
Meaning

We start the course with the invitation to be present. This moment is here, waiting to be engaged with and we don't want you to miss it. We ask you not to be doing anything else when you are being with – resist the urge to check emails or text messages; where possible, if you are joining online, try to keep your camera on so others can see you present with them. Even deeper than these simple acts of generosity, we invite you to start to imagine what it would be like to step away from the things that preoccupy our minds with the past or the future. You are invited to truly live, here and now, to truly be with yourself, with others and the world around you and with God.

Welcome

We start each week with a welcome question for each person to respond to when they are ready. Today's is:

What has brought you to this course?

People have different reasons for doing this course and I hope you will quickly learn that there are no wrong answers here. Some of you may have had an experience that makes you wonder about what you believe about God and the meaning of life – a baby is born or you have a brush with death when you or someone close becomes ill. You want to live more purposefully and to work out what you want to look back at at the end of life and be glad you lived by.

For others it may be about a person, someone in your life who has caught your imagination by what their faith means to them. It might be your partner, it might be someone at work or a friend or family member, but you want to understand what makes them tick and you are open to participating in their faith if you can find a way to do it that is authentic to you.

For others it may be about belonging. You've realized that you feel on the edge of society or your church. Perhaps you've decided you want to do something about feeling isolated. This is a great reason to connect here. Perhaps it was because something has happened, you realized something about yourself or you have experienced something other people in your community have not experienced. This course is also for you if you want to rediscover your faith in your circumstances rather than lose it because you don't fit in with what works for other people in following God.

The welcome question each week is an invitation to *be with* yourself, where you are now, and this week it is an invitation to be with whatever is the reason you have arrived in this group.

It is also an invitation to hold other people's reasons as a gift – so we ask you not to comment or offer advice on others' reasons. The host will offer a simple 'Thank you' on behalf of the group for each contribution.

Wonderings

The wonderings part of the course continues this commitment to receiving what each other offers without judgement – even positive judgement – but simply as a gift.

The host will continue to offer a simple, two-word 'Thank you' on behalf of the group, and this is the only response that will be said to each contribution. It is fine to contribute by listening attentively if you'd rather not speak.

Every week there will be a series of wonderings. We call them 'wonderings' not 'questions' because a question can have a right or wrong answer, but an invitation to wonder with us is an invitation to go wherever these prompts take you. This may sound rather risky. Who knows where this group will go? But this is the point: we want to journey with you; so each group has a slightly different experience of this course because each group is different. You make a difference with your experiences, your interests and your personality. And so does everyone else. The role of the hosts is to bring out the best of that rather than squeeze everyone into a mould.

Here are the wonderings for this week:

- *I wonder if you've known what it feels like to be set free.*
- *I wonder if you've known what it feels like to be in prison.*
- *I wonder what it's like to know there's something in the past that you don't need to worry about anymore.*
- *I wonder what it would be like to know the future isn't going to hurt you.*

Talk Introduction

We've spent some time sharing the truth, beauty and meaning we have discovered through our life events and listening to those of others in the group. This is often the heart of the course, and the method of receiving everything that is contributed as a simple gift means that we have the opportunity to connect with the most meaningful experiences in the lives of people who may be very different from us. However, we are still likely to find that everyone in our group is similar in some ways. They may live in one country or one area or all share certain experiences of life. How do we ensure that the faith we are exploring is not just a reflection of this?

Sam Wells, who co-created this course, is widely recognized for developing the theology of what he calls 'being with'. He has explored this with theorists and practitioners across the world and throughout history. The talks he's written for this course seek to bring our experiences into conversation with ideas that have been discussed in other places and at other times.

The talks are not intended to correct the contributions you have offered in the wondering time, but to be in conversation with them. You may hear the storyteller mention your contribution if it speaks to a particular part of the talk that week.

Talk: Meaning

The present tense doesn't exist. Try to put your finger on it, and whoosh – it's gone. There's no such thing as the present tense.

As soon as we realize this, we become subject to two primal terrors. The first terror is this: you can't stop time. It's out of control. The second terror is this: what we've done can't be undone. However much we try to airbrush the photographs, or fiddle with the timings on the emails, there's no changing what's happened.

> And these two terrors – the panic about the past and the fear of the future – together constitute the prison of human existence.

And these two terrors – the panic about the past and the fear of the future – together constitute the prison of human existence. There's no genuine living in the present tense because

4

our lives are dominated by regret and bitterness about the past, and are paralysed by fear and anxiety about the future. Think about what grieves us. It's what's happened in the past that we can't change, the sequence of events that's led to a kind of prison, to our being in some sense in chains. It's the things we cherish that we dread we can't keep – our youth, our life, the things and the people we love; this very moment right now.

And what does the Christian faith proclaim? Two central convictions: one about the past; and one about the future.

Forgiveness

The first conviction is about the past. It's forgiveness. Forgiveness doesn't change the things that cause us regret or bitterness. But it releases us from the power of the past. Forgiveness doesn't rewrite history. But it prevents our histories asphyxiating us. Forgiveness transforms our past from an enemy to a friend, from a horror-show of shame to a storehouse of wisdom. In the absence of forgiveness, we're isolated from our past, trying pitifully to bury or destroy the many things that haunt, overshadow, plague and torment us. Forgiveness doesn't change these things but it does change their relationship to us. No longer do they imprison us, pursue us, surround us or stalk us. Now they accompany us, deepen us, teach us, train us. Nothing, in the end, is wasted. That's the work of forgiveness. It's about the transformation of the prison of the past.

> Forgiveness transforms our past from an enemy to a friend.

Imagine being released from the prison of the past. It's almost beyond our imaginations. It's half of Christianity.

Everlasting life

The second conviction is about the future. The life everlasting. Everlasting life doesn't take away the unknown element of the future but it does take away the paroxysm of fear that engulfs the cloud of unknowing. Everlasting life doesn't dismantle the reality of death, suffering, bereavement but it does offer life beyond death, comfort beyond suffering, companionship beyond separation. In the absence of everlasting life, we're terrified of our future, perpetually trying to secure permanence in the face of change, meaning in the face of waste, distraction in the face of despair. Everlasting life doesn't undermine human endeavour but it does rid it of the last word; evil is real but it won't have the final say; death is coming but it doesn't obliterate the power of God; identity is fragile but that in us which resides in God will be changed into glory.

Imagine for a moment the gift of everlasting life. Feel it slowly dismantle all your worst fears. Let it set you free. Let it give you indescribable joy. It's the other half of Christianity.

The heart of it all is forgiveness and everlasting life. If you have those, nothing can finally hurt you.

Now, for the first time, we can have a present tense – we can experience the present without being tense. The past, what we trust God has done, we call faith. The future, what we believe God will do, we call hope. The present, what God embodies and makes possible, we call love.

Response

What is your response to this week? Here is some space to note things you don't want to forget and any reflections or questions you would like to take to next week's session.

_____

_____

_____

_____

_____

_____

Week Two
Essence

Welcome

Now we are into the course we will bring in the same welcome question each week. This way you know it is coming and can be thinking about what you'll share. The question we will ask you every week from now on, the question we think most helps you to be with yourself in the here and now present is this:

What has been the heart of your week?

This is an invitation to scan over the last seven days and think of something that has happened that has stayed with you through the other times. It is an invitation to share an event or experience from your week that you hold in you right now.

Wonderings

Learning to be with another person while they are sharing is a muscle we need to exercise before it comes naturally. For most of us, it is far easier to leap in with words: 'I know just how you feel' or 'That's nothing compared to what happened to me' or 'Have you thought about fixing it with …?' While all these responses can be very helpful in regular conversation, and they're not wrong, in this course we are investing not just in hearing about being with but in training in practices that help us to enter into being with as a way of life. Just as we may do things at the gym or in an exercise class that we wouldn't do at work or in the high street, because they train our muscles to be stronger in everyday life, we practise behaviours in a controlled environment so that we may be able to experience a concentrated version of being with each other so that we can grow this muscle for everyday life. It isn't a big deal if you or someone makes a mistake, just as it's not a big deal if you make a wrong move in an exercise class. Most groups take a week or two to get the hang of not responding to contributions but receiving them in silence as mysterious gifts from the heart of another person. But we need to get into the practice if we are to enter into this course. We believe people are a mystery to be entered into, not a problem to be solved: this includes you and this includes God.

Here are the wonderings for this week:

- *I wonder where you find most meaning in life.*
- *I wonder if there's an idea that encapsulates what you think life is all about.*
- *Tell about a time you wanted something to last for ever.*
- *I wonder what's the best thing in life.*

Talk Introduction

This course approaches discussions from a variety of different ways because we are aware that people have different ways to discover things. This week is a particularly philosophical take. Don't worry if you don't follow every line of the talk. Our talks are designed to have enough so that everyone in the group can catch something and then share it with the group later. This way we all need each other to understand more about God. It's the only way a group of people can grow in understanding about God. There isn't one message you are supposed to learn from each talk, so listen for something that connects with you and there may be something someone else brings later that helps you to grasp another point. This course is about transformation not just information, and for that we need to learn from each other, not simply find all the answers ourselves.

Talk: Essence

There are two kinds of things: those that abide for ever; those that last for a limited time. The things that abide for ever we call essence; the things that last for a shorter period we call existence.

Existence

We human beings are in the second, shorter-period category. We exist: we think that because we exist, we're the heart of all things. But we forget that existence isn't all there is. We're missing something: something vital. Existence is not the same as essence. Existence is subject to change, decay and death. Essence isn't. Yes, we do exist. But we're not essences: we're not permanent. We're not essential. Take us away and there still is. Our being depends on the existence of others. We crave independence but independence is an illusion: we never could be independent; and there would be no joy in being so. The longing for independence is the aspiration to be an essence: the secret of happiness is to learn instead to exist.

Why are we here? We exist because the essence of all things, in the depths of its mysteries, brought into being something that was not essential, something ... else. We're part of that 'else'. There could have been no existence. There could have been nothing beyond essence. Yet here we are. We're lost in wonder at the transition from eternity to time, from boundlessness to circumscription, from the elusive and immortal to the tangible and fragile. We're bursting with gratitude when we realize that there's nothing whatsoever for which we can claim the credit.

Essence

And here, in the depths of wonder, we meet the astonishing claim of the Christian faith. On one starry night, displaced by migration, in a hostile political climate, surrounded by animals, from a young mother living homeless in a strange town, *essence entered existence*. Essence, which we could call by a hundred names but most often call God; essence, which could have remained alone without ever conceiving of existence; essence, which would most straightforwardly have left things as nothing but out of utmost grace, initiated existence –

> In Jesus, *the essence of all things became part of existence* – subject to change, decay and death, just like us.

that essence made itself part of existence. The Word became flesh. In Jesus, *the essence of all things became part of existence* – subject to change, decay and death, just like us.

Here we discover the answer to perhaps the biggest question of all: why is there something rather than nothing? The answer is because essence, or God as we usually say, always intended to be our companion, to be with us. That's what the word 'Jesus' represents: God's eternal purpose to be with us, which triggered the whole mystery of existence from beginning to end. Jesus isn't an afterthought that entered existence when essence realized existence was going badly wrong: *Jesus is the whole meaning and purpose for existence in the first place.* Jesus is the reason we exist.

Eternal truth

But we haven't yet reached the best bit. Here we come to the most astonishing wonder of all. Jesus is fully human and fully divine – complete existence, utter essence. And through him we realize what God's final purpose always was: *to bring us into essence* – into eternal truth. Jesus is God stretching out a hand and saying, 'Come into the essence of all things to be with me.' Remember the painting of God and Adam on the roof of the Sistine Chapel in the Vatican in Rome? God's hand is stretched out in creation. But the final purpose of creation is that God's hand stretches out a second time, in Jesus, and *invites us to become part of the very essence of all things.* What an inexpressible gift.

And so here we are – tiny, pointless, transient specks in the inconceivable enormity of space–time existence. But the personal quality of essence, which we call God, has chosen to enter existence, and become one of us, because of a primordial desire to be with us, in tender, understanding, gentle, humble relationship with us; and that's the reason for existence in the first place. And this being with, which we call Jesus, sets forth a capacity to live in this relationship henceforth, a capacity we call the Holy Spirit; and the ultimate purpose is for God not just to share existence with us, but to draw us finally into essence, and dwell with us for ever, even when all existence has passed away. And so every time we form, establish, restore and deepen tender, understanding, gentle, humble relationship with one another, like we're doing right now, we imitate and anticipate the way God seeks to be with us, and glimpse the glory of eternity.

Response

What is your response to this week? Here is some space to note things you don't want to forget and any reflections or questions you would like to take to next week's session.

_____

_____

_____

_____

_____

_____

_____

Week Three
Jesus

Welcome

We hope you're now getting the hang of the being with way of receiving contributions from others, listening without judgement or comparison. So let's look at what we ask each week in our welcome.

What has been the heart of your week?

This is very deliberately not 'What was the highlight of your week?' This is not aimed at getting you to brighten the day of the others in your group. It's OK to say something that was not good or positive. We hope you feel safe to share whatever was authentically the heart of your week, including if you felt exhausted, broke up with your girl-friend or had a bad meeting at work. It can be large or small because we are made up not just of life-changing events, but also of small highs and lows. Being with ourselves and inviting others to be with us as we honestly are at this point in time is at the heart of entering into the being-with mindset. It is entirely up to you how much you want to share with your group, and you can say you have had a difficult week without going into much detail if you would prefer. But by now, all being well, you are discovering trust being built in your group. Sharing our authentic selves can mean that others can respond with the gentleness you may need this week, or understand if you don't say much.

Wonderings

Normally in the wonderings we stick to language that isn't religious but this week we invite you to wonder about Jesus. There are no wrong answers to wonderings. Don't feel that these wonderings are only for others. The aim of this course is to start where you are but it is also to open up what you have that is already able to engage with the person at the heart of the Christian faith. If you don't feel you know as much about Jesus as some in your group, don't be put off – often fresh thinking brings something without cliché, a new insight that the whole group benefits from or an honest response that means others can be honest too.

Here are the wonderings for this week:

- *I wonder who you'd say 'your people' are.*
- *I wonder who you feel Jesus' people are.*
- *Tell about a time you found solidarity with an unexpected group of people.*
- *I wonder if there's any way you feel Jesus was like you.*

Talk Introduction

Like the wonderings, this week's talk invites us into the world of Jesus. Most of the talks in this course are comfortably within language you would be used to if you have no background in discussing faith but this week we invite you into the time and space when Jesus was on earth. I know it's only Week Three but the heart of the being with idea is that God joined humanity at a particular point in history, with a particular group of people. Like watching a film or reading a book set in another time or place, there is cultural language related to that world. As we take seriously that Jesus existed not in the abstract but in language and culture that is as important as our own, we invite you to hear about that world in its own terms rather than just as an extension of our concepts and language.

Here are some of the words that you may be less familiar with:

- The word *gospel* simply means Good News or Good Story. It was used in the first century at the start of public announcements of things like a public holiday or to say an official was coming to visit.
- *Good Friday* is the day Christians call the day Jesus died, marked each year just before Easter.
- *Nazareth* was the working-class town where Jesus grew up.
- *Discipleship* is about learning how to be a follower of Jesus.

You can see this talk as a hand, open in front of us, offering to lead us down the path of learning to consciously be disciples of Jesus. It may be that you've been following Jesus' way of living for a while. It may be that you haven't. This week we invite you to think about what being a disciple of Jesus could mean in your life. And what it doesn't mean.

Talk: Jesus

The gospel story is, in fact, three interwoven stories:

- The first is Jesus' creation of a new community, based around the hopes of his words and actions. He calls around him 12 companions and commissions them to spread the fire of his message. The companions falter and stumble, out of fear of suffering, lack of imagination and cold betrayal. But in the resurrection there's promise of a restored community to live his life and share his truth.
- The second is Jesus' mission to the crowd, the teeming mass of the oppressed, who are mentioned over and over again in the story of Jesus' life. This is a ministry of healing, teaching and liberation, through story, announcement and gesture. When Jesus enters Jerusalem on a donkey, the crowd seems to have taken up the cause of liberation. But by Good Friday they've chosen a terrorist called Barabbas instead.
- The third is Jesus' confrontation with the leaders who held Israel in a stranglehold. One by one Jesus takes on each of the rulers and religious leaders. He dismantles their authority and challenges their control. But eventually the veil is pulled aside, and behind it is revealed the real power in the land, which toys with all other powers – the iron fist of Rome. It's the nails and wood of Roman execution that finally destroy Jesus – only for him to dismantle even Rome's control over life and death.

These three threads – of companions, crowd and authorities – are interwoven in Jesus' story like three strands in a rope. Each finds its climax in the account of Jesus' death. The three stories in the end comprise one story. Jesus' intimacy with his companions, his mission to the crowd and his confrontation with the authorities are all dimensions of his being at the heart of God.

Our story

This story is our story. Our story divides into the same three strands as Jesus' story – companionship, issues of poverty, and conflict.

- First, we're part of a group of companions. A Christian is called into relationship with a community. We may already have close family ties, and our call to follow the man from Nazareth may intensify and strengthen these existing relationships or it may test and challenge them. But either way, we're called to make new, close and accountable relationships with members of Christ's church.
- Second, we're in relationship with those who are oppressed. There are many ways to do this. The relationship that brings about real change is friendship because to be a friend is to say, 'I am allowing myself to be changed by knowing you.'
- Third, we attend to Jesus' confrontation with the authorities of his day. Jesus is continually having heated debates with everyone who held the nation in check. The one thing everyone seems to agree on today is that there's plenty wrong with the world. There are only two responses to this – either go and put it right yourself or, if you can't, make life pretty uncomfortable for those who can until they do.

And just as for Jesus' story, these three strands – of accountable community, friendship with those who have their backs to the wall and challenge to the powerful – all unite in the fundamental story, which is our commissioning by God, our sharing in the of mystery of God and our entering the glory of God. Jesus' relationship with God was expressed, discovered and revealed through accountable community, friendship with those who have their backs to the wall and challenge to the powerful. Why should ours be any different?

Living the story

Our temptation is trying to have the big story, walking with God, without the stories that make up the big story – participation in an accountable community, friendship with those who have their backs to the wall and challenge to the powerful. Our temptation is wanting to have all the benefits of Christian faith without any of the costs. Our temptation is trying to have God without Jesus.

> Our temptation is wanting to have all the benefits of Christian faith without any of the costs.

But there's another side to the coin. Getting any one of the strands out of proportion is also a temptation. Look at accountable community. We can easily fall into thinking that's all that matters. We can surround ourselves with people like us. It's the same in regard to friendship with the oppressed. Discipleship isn't a lone quest. When we've discovered the depth of human need, we don't just give in to the temptation of anger or despair, but gather a community of partners and confront those who maintain a pattern of oppression. Again, in relation to challenging the powerful, we mustn't fall into thinking that there's always a simple explanation and the powerful are always to blame. We mustn't assume there's a theory that justifies our anger if such a theory tempts us to neglect our own friendship with the poor and commitment to accountable community.

All of these are temptations to have just part of the gospel – just the community bit, just the oppression bit or just the cage-rattling bit – without the rest. You could say they are temptations to remake Jesus in the image of our own needs and obsessions. They take one of the three strands and ignore the big story. It's the temptation to have Jesus without God.

The gospel leaves us with these three questions:

- Am I a disciple? – That is, am I member of a group of people that holds me to account and challenges me to put my life where my mouth is?
- Am I a friend of those who have their backs to the wall? Have I said to a single person, for whom life is a daily struggle and burden, 'I am allowing myself to be changed by knowing you'?
- Am I confronting oppression? Am I a thorn in the side of those who abuse and manipulate and extort and neglect? Or does the way I spend my money and the lifestyle I unthinkingly adopt simply underwrite and collude in patterns of exploitation and degradation?

These are three questions that put feet on the gospel.

Response

What is your response to this week? Here is some space to note things you don't want to forget and any reflections or questions you would like to take to next week's session.

_____

_____

_____

_____

_____

_____

Week Four
Church

Welcome

As we continue to practise this model of being with together you are invited to look for things that delight you about your fellow participants. Your group will include people who are different from you and we invite you to enjoy each other. People can share things that are deeply painful and unresolved in this course and this is not in conflict with discovering that you enjoy spending time with them. You may find yourself valuing something in the way they talk about things or who they are. Take note of this – give yourself time to feel that value of them. The practice of not being able to respond with words can feel passive. However, as we enter into it fully we discover that it is anything but passive. It is truly engaging.

What has been the heart of your week?

Wonderings

Christianity is a team sport. There are no lone-ranger followers of Jesus. Even those who don't go to church regularly are part of an unseen community that has influenced them and who they influence by their presence or absence. But our experiences of communities, including Christian communities, don't always seem to reflect Christianity's founder. Equally, our experiences of community outside of religious settings can teach us a lot about what community can be at its best. So this week we are invited to bring our experiences of community together, good and bad and hold space for those who have different experiences from us.

Here are the wonderings for this week:

- *Tell about a community that you've been part of.*
  - *Tell about the ways it brought out the best in you and others.*
  - *Tell about the ways it relished difference and diversity.*
  - *Tell about the ways it addressed failure or undermining actions.*
- *I wonder what kinds of qualities a community needs to be sustainable.*
- *I wonder what kinds of qualities you believe you bring to a community.*

Talk Introduction

Have you noticed that your storyteller has a habit of weaving your wonderings into the talk? This is based on one of the key beliefs that underpin the Being With course: the belief that God is at work in everyone's lives from day one, not just the so-called 'religious' folk. God is generous: you have truth, beauty and meaning in your life as much as anyone, and this can help you and others in your group as you explore faith. We also don't own all the truth about God. As we hear talks with insights taken from thinking about God being with us that go back two thousand years, our contributions have a place too. This is supposed to be less of a talk and more of a conversation, listening well and including your insights. We wanted this course to reflect the idea of *partnership*. We invite you not to sit quietly and hear the truth from us, but to partner with us in discovering something new together. Each Being With course is different because each group is different. Each group needs each member to be all they can be. We hope you've spotted that in being with each other on this course we are, together, building a shared experience of what it means to be church.

Talk: Church

There was once a pastor who had an unusual way of finishing the Sunday service. He would bow down to the congregation. He used to say, 'Some clergy bow before the holy table and some bow before the cross. But I'm told that these people are the body of Christ, so I bow before them.' Paul tells us that each member of the church is like an eye, an ear or a hand in the same body. The foot can't say to the hand, 'I don't need you', nor can the eye say to the rest, 'I'm the whole body.' And Paul underlines that the weaker members of the body are vital to its health and welfare. What does Paul mean?

> Paul tells us that each member of the church is like an eye or an ear or a hand in the same body.

Richard Adams' 1972 novel *Watership Down* tells the story of a dozen rabbits that search for a warren to call home. Each of the communities the rabbits encounter has its own political system.

- The first warren at the beginning of the novel is like a traditional, hierarchical society. The rabbits run away from that warren because they correctly anticipate it's about to be destroyed by humans.
- A second warren the rabbits meet is run on a totalitarian model. There's one general who keeps all the other rabbits in a state of fear under a military regime.
- A third community of rabbits seems to resemble a modern decadent society. The rabbits there are somewhat inebriated. Food is plentiful and the living is easy. But the rabbits have lost the ability to

find their own food and, more seriously, to tell the truth. They can't bring themselves to acknowledge that they're under the spell of a farmer who feeds them but also snares and kills them one by one.

- The fourth warren is the one the rabbits found for themselves on *Watership Down*.

The rabbits discover a great many things through their travels and adventures. The most important thing they discover is that they need each other. One of the rabbits is big and strong; another is quick thinking and imaginative; a third is speedy; a fourth is fiercely loyal; a fifth is a good storyteller. The key rabbit is the smallest and clumsiest, who yet has a sixth sense that anticipates danger – like the destruction of the original warren. What makes this group of rabbits so significant is that they find ways of using the gifts of every member of the party so that they're never short of wisdom and intelligence about what to do next or courage and strength to do what's needed. In other words, the group of rabbits lives and moves and thinks as one body rather than as a dozen separate bodies. There can't be such a thing as an idea or a development that is good for one of the rabbits but not good for the whole body.

This group of rabbits offers us three lessons about what it might mean to be church:

- First, we can never say we've 'made it'. The rabbits in the story are longing to get to the point where they can say, 'Phew – that's it. We've made it.' Well, there is no such point. The moment never comes. When the dozen refugees meet the easy-living rabbits enjoying the good life, they can see quite quickly that those inebriated rabbits have lost what it takes to be a community, to tell the truth and ultimately to survive. The disciples were formed on the way from Galilee to Jerusalem. The church becomes one body as it's bound together on its common journey. It's always a work in progress.
- Second, the diversity of the church is a strength, not a weak-

ness. The group of rabbits only survived because it had rabbits with different gifts, different strengths, different visions for what they were doing and where they were going. Paul says there are varieties of gifts but the same Spirit; varieties of ways of serving God but the same Lord.

Once, there was a monastery where the monks were continually at each other's throats, bickering and cursing at one another. One night a mysterious visitor knocked at the monastery door and made a brief but solemn announcement: 'One of you is Jesus Christ.' The atmosphere in the monastery changed overnight. Suddenly each monk treated every other monk with awe and wonder, not sure which one was Jesus but knowing Jesus was among them. They'd learnt what it means to be church – to treat one another as we would treat Jesus.

The Bible is made up of 66 books. Each is different, and one or two even seem to contradict one another. If we take it for granted that these 66 books work together to reveal God, why can't we take it for granted that different kinds of churches can also be places where God is made known? We need each other to know God. We cannot say to one another, 'I have no need of you.'

- Third, being one body isn't just a matter of ignoring differences. The rabbits of *Watership Down* don't deny their diversity – allowing tolerance to break out and dimming the lights to a point where they are all grey. What saves the rabbits at crucial moments is their willingness and commitment to listen to one another, to hear each other out when they have stories, worries, misgivings or hopes. Out of these curious memories and visions come the gifts that make the group of rabbits so resilient and so adaptable. Paul's picture isn't about bland tolerance. It's about shared direction, wisdom and pain. Being one body is probably more painful than going our separate ways. We spend a lot of our time searching around for vital things we have to do that make listening to one

25

another's stories seem like a waste of time. But Paul says to us. 'Your mission is to be one body. Your message is that Christ has made you one body. There isn't anything more important for you to rush off to.' Telling another Christian 'I have no need of you' is really telling Jesus, 'I have no need of you.'

Response

If you're not a regular churchgoer at this point in your life, we'd like to invite you to take this opportunity and what you've learned this week and try out a church service this weekend. It may be the church running this course or a church local to where you live. There may be others in your group who would like to do this with you and you could go together. You can also share your experiences of this with your group next week and have a chance to ask any questions, to process what you enjoyed or what you found challenging. If you start now and like it there will be time to go regularly while you are exploring your faith with the support of this group.

What is your response to this week? Here is some space to note things you don't want to forget and any reflections or questions you would like to take to next week's session.

_____

_____

_____

_____

_____

_____

_____

Week Five
Bible

Welcome

This course is based around the invitation to tell stories. Stories are different from facts in that they involve a person. Hearing that I, Sally, am 5 foot 2 inches doesn't tell you about my experience of the world as a relatively short person. It doesn't tell you that there are advantages to being on the smaller side and that there are times I quite enjoy it. Simply hearing the facts doesn't tell you about me. The same is true with others. Giving time to hear the stories that make up the other people in your group is saying that you value them as a person. It is also true for yourself. Stopping to think about the stories that you hold, that make you who you are, and experiencing others give attention to those without judgement, is a way to learn to be with yourself.

What has been the heart of your week?

Wonderings

- *Tell about a story you've loved a long time.*
- *Tell about a story concerning your family that everyone has heard too many times.*
- *I wonder if you've ever felt there was a story that had no place for you.*

- *I wonder if you've ever felt there was a story that did have a place for you.*

Talk Introduction

Stories are also how we are invited to discover God. The Bible is made up of stories of God engaging with particular people in particular cultures and situations. Our talk this week seeks to give us a map so that we can see where those stories fit and how we can find our place in the ongoing love story of God with humanity.

Sam conceives of the great story of God as a play with five acts. Here are some concepts that may be new as you're hearing it:

- The word 'Israel' refers to the descendants of a man called Abraham who you'll hear about in today's talk.
- You may recognize the phrase 'pleased to dwell' from the carol 'Hark the Herald Angels Sing', which covers the same ideas.
- Jerusalem was the capital city of the region where Jesus was killed.
- Crucifixion – a drawn-out, humiliating death, stripped naked and hung above the ground with nails pressed through flesh into pieces of wood.
- While Christians believe that Jesus is God become human and, like us, in one point and time, the Holy Spirit is God mobile and flexible, with the world, healing and encouraging, challenging and guiding Jesus' followers (and everyone else, including you, from the first moment you were alive).
- Christians also believe that one day *Jesus will return* to remake the world and start life beyond time where there is no death or injustice. We talk about this in Act Five.
- 'God's sovereignty' refers to the authority and power of God to make decisions.

Talk: Bible

The Bible tells a story in five acts:

- *The first act is creation.* There was too much love in God for God not to share it. The world isn't the centre of the story; God is. Things do not have to be the way they are - they exist because God chose for them to be. God is the creator, and God is surrounded by creatures. Those creatures do not exist for themselves but have a purpose for God. God made them this way because God wanted one like each of them. Their chief purpose is to glorify and enjoy God for ever. And yet these creatures use their freedom badly. They choose, but have lost the art of making good choices. God pours out just as much love as before but so little is returned; so much creative, playful, joyful energy is wasted. Here's the drama of creation, of how God came to turn infinite, divine freedom into a covenant, and how humanity comes to turn finite, created freedom into a prison.
- *The second act is Israel.* God longed to be in true relationship with creation through the part of creation that recognized the divine glory - humankind. God called a man called Abraham, and Abraham followed. The rest of the Old Testament is a love story in which Abraham's descendants strive with God, unable to live with God and unable to live without God. God will not leave them alone: therein lies a promise and a warning. The nation that grew from Abraham exists for God and for the salvation of the nations. Can they find the forms of life that honour its call to be holy? How will God woo or wrest them back when they stray? How far is too far to stray? Will God save the nations another way?
- *The third act is Jesus.* This is the definitive act, at the centre of the drama, in which God's character is revealed; the author enters

29

the drama. In Jesus all the fullness of God was pleased to dwell. There's constantly a human level of encounter, of intimacy and betrayal, of challenge and confrontation. But there's also a cosmic dimension of the magnetism of Jerusalem, the inevitability of his death, the inability of the grave to keep him down. Is God totally vulnerable or has something been kept back? Will God's people understand, comprehend and follow, or will they seek to overcome, stand over, obliterate and annihilate? Will their rejection of God cause God's rejection of them? If God overcomes death, what will God not do?

- *Christians are in Act Four, the church.* In this act, the church is given all it needs to continue to be Christ's body in the world. It receives the Holy Spirit and is clothed with power and authority. It is given the Scripture, made up of the apostolic witness of those who seek to report the drama, while being drawn it, the drama. It is given baptism. It is given the Eucharist, a regular event in which the body of Christ meets the embodied Christ, in a drama of encounter, reconciliation and commission. It is given a host of other practices to form and sustain its life. Will those gifts prove to be enough? Will the church seek solace elsewhere? Will the ways God speaks and acts beyond the church prove more vivid than the ways God's voice is heard and God's deeds are perceived within?
- *Act Five brings the end.* This is a frightening thing for those who have built up power and resources, but for those who have nothing to lose it is unbounded joy. The timing of the end is not known, but that it will come when God chooses is certain. The drama of that time may yield some shocks – as the secrets of all hearts are revealed. But in God's revelation there will be no shocks, only surprises. For the God who will then be fully revealed will not be different in character from the God who was revealed in Act Three. The face on the cross is the face on the throne.

There are two kinds of mistakes that can easily be made about this five-act drama:

- *The first mistake is to think we're in a one-act play rather than a five-act play.* The world – all that has taken God's freedom not yet to believe – thinks it's in a one-act play. In a one-act play, all meanings must be established before the curtain comes down. This life is all there is: heritage has no logical value other than insofar as it contributes to fulfilment here and now. All achievements, all results, all outcomes must be celebrated and resolved before the final whistle. The five-act drama means that Christians are spared such a crisis. They're not called to be effective or successful, but to be faithful. Faithfulness is effectiveness measured against a much longer timescale: since Act Three has happened and Act Five is to follow, Christians can afford to fail because they trust in Christ's victory and in God's ultimate sovereignty. Their faithful failures point all the more to their faith in their story and its author.
- *The second mistake is to get the wrong act.* This overemphasizes our own role in the drama. If we assume we're in Act One, we place ourselves, rather than God, in the role of creator. There have been no significant events before our appearance in the drama. There's no experience to learn from, no story to join, no drama to enter. This is the desire for independence, to be a self-made individual. No one else's rules have validity: everything must be discovered, named, assessed for ourselves. Similar is the assumption that we are at the end of the story. This is as much the case in the church, thinking it is in Act Five, as in the world, taking itself to be near the end of a one-act play. On the great debating points of church order, people talk as if Jesus and the early church lived an eternity ago, and that they set everything in stone. But what if Jesus lives today, and the church still has thousands or millions of years ahead of it? Perhaps we *are* the early church, still haggling over

the details, and rightly so. On nuclear weapons or climate change, people similarly assume that they are near the end of the story. Blowing up the world would indeed be terrible. But the five-act drama proclaims that humanity has already, in Act Three, done the most terrible thing possible by crucifying the Lord of glory. And a proper understanding of God's sovereignty recognizes that God could well have another world, in all the myriad complexities of this one, all ready and prepared, on hand to replace this one should there ever be a need. Humans are not the creators, nor the finishers, of God's story.

Response

What is your response to this week? Here is some space to note things you don't want to forget and any reflections or questions you would like to take to next week's session.

_____

_____

_____

_____

_____

_____

_____

Week Six
Mission

Welcome

What has been the heart of your week?

Wonderings

- *Tell about an occasion when someone has been so keen to fix you that they've missed a moment when you just wanted to be heard and understood.*
- *Tell about when you worked on a project with a group of people and got satisfaction from achieving it.*
- *I wonder if you've ever wanted to tell someone to stop moaning about a problem and go and do something about it.*
- *Tell about a time when someone truly heard, understood and cared about you in the midst of a crisis.*

Talk Introduction

Now we've got to know you, we are going to be completely transparent in what we hope we are doing with this course and what we aim to do in everything as we interact with the wider world.

It's important as you hear this to know what we're *not* saying. This course has a particular focus on being with but it doesn't mean to say that other things are wrong. Jesus spent time *doing* things *with* his followers and together they healed the sick and taught about God; and Jesus spent some time *doing* things *for* humanity in his suffering and death. If Jesus did things for us and with us, then they have to be good too. But this course hopes to show that undergirding all of this is a commitment to be with us. We are also invited to live with being with as the focus, even if we are also doing things for or with or being for others. God has no other goal for you that is more important than simply being with you. Everything else is detail.

Talk: Mission

'With' is the most important word in the Christian faith. Let's explore four models of social engagement:

- *Working for* is where *I* do things and they make *your* life better. Working for is the established model of social engagement. It takes for granted that the way to address disadvantage or distress is for those with skills, knowledge, energy and resources to enhance the situation of those who are struggling. It assumes the advantaged have abundance, which defines them: they should maximize that surplus through education and training; and exercise it through applying their skills broadly. By contrast, the 'needy' are defined by their deficit; if they have capacities, these are seldom noticed or harnessed. Working for identifies problems, focusing on the ones it has the skills and interest to fix. It then moves on to address further such problems, of which the world is never short. It seldom stops to ask why the recipients of such corrective measures are invariably so ungrateful.

- *Working with* is a different model. Like working for, it gains its energy from problem-solving, identifying targets, overcoming obstacles and feeding off the bursts of energy that result. Working for assumes the concentration of power in the expert and the highly skilled. By contrast, working with locates power in coalitions of interest: initially collectives of the like-minded and similarly socially located, but eventually partnerships around common causes, across conventional divides of religion and class. Its stumbling blocks are not the maladies working for identifies; they are pessimism, apathy, timidity, lack of confidence and discouragement. Working with forms networks and creates a movement where all stakeholders come together and it's possible for everyone to win. Thus it establishes momentum and empowers the dispossessed.

- *Being with* begins by largely rejecting the problem–solution axis that dominates both the previous models. Its main concern is the predicament that has no solution – the scenario that can't be fixed. It sees the vast majority of life, and certainly the most significant moments of life, in these terms: love can't be achieved; death can't be fixed; pregnancy and birth aren't a problem needing a solution. When it comes to social engagement, it believes you can seldom solve people's problems. Doing so disempowers them and reinforces their low social standing. Instead, you must accompany people while they find their own methods, answers, approaches. Meanwhile you can celebrate and enjoy the rest of their identity that's not wrapped up in what you (perhaps ignorantly) judge to be their problem. Like working with, being with starts with people's assets, not their deficits. It seeks never to do for them what they can perfectly well, perhaps with encouragement and support, do for themselves. But most importantly, being with seeks to model the goal of all relationships. It sees problem-solving as a means to a perpetually deferred end. Instead it tries to live that end – enjoying people for their own sake.

• *Being for* is the philosophy that's more concerned with getting the ideas right. It strives to use the right language and have the right attitudes. It wants to ensure products are sustainably sourced and investments ethically funded, people are described in positive ways, and accountable public action is firmly distinguished from private consumer choice. Much of this is good; but in its clamour that Something Must Be Done, it invariably becomes apparent that it's for somebody else to do the doing. The alternative to unwise action becomes not engaged presence but cynical withdrawal: multiple causes are advanced, but their untidy details and complexities are often disdained. In an information-saturated, instantly judging, observer-shaped internet age, it's the default position of perhaps the majority.

Jesus works for us by forgiving sins and opening the gates of everlasting life – achievements concentrated in his suffering, death and resurrection and anticipated in earlier healings and miracles. But Jesus also spends perhaps three years, largely in the north eastern province of Galilee: there he is calling, forming and empowering followers, formulating a message for them to share, building alliances and confronting hostility. One can see the 'saving' as working for, focused on a week in Jerusalem; and the 'organizing' as working with, spread over those years of public ministry. But that still leaves perhaps 30 years in Nazareth, give or take a spell as a baby in Egypt. And here's the question: if Jesus was all about working for, how come he spent around 90 per cent being with (in Nazareth), 9 per cent working with (in Galilee) – and only 1 per cent working for (in Jerusalem). Are those percentages significant – and do they provide a template for Christian mission? Surely Jesus knew what he was doing in the way he spent his time; or do we know better?

We can identify eight dimensions of what being with actually involves. Here are three of the eight:

- One is *mystery*. This rests on distinguishing between a *problem*, which has a generic quality, can be perceived equally well by anybody, can be addressed from the outside and can be solved using skills acquired elsewhere, and a *mystery*, which is unique, can't be fixed or broken down into its constituent parts, is not fully apparent to an outsider and can only be entered, explored and appreciated.
- Another is *delight*. This is the recognition of abundance where conventional engagement is inclined only to see deficit. Delight rejects the template of how things should be and opens itself to surprise, humour, subversion and playfulness. Delight is glad to take time where conventional engagement is overshadowed by urgency. It sees assets where conventional judgement focuses on deficits.
- The seventh dimension, which encapsulates and epitomizes all the previous ones, is *enjoyment*. This rests on Augustine's distinction between what we *use*, which runs out and is a means to some further end, and what we *enjoy*, which is of value for its own sake, an end in itself. Being with, simply put, is enjoying people whom the world, having no use for, is inclined to discard.

And so we come to the heart of this course. For by practising being with one another, we discover what it means to be with God.

Response

What is your response to this week? Here is some space to note things you don't want to forget and any reflections or questions you would like to take to next week's session.

_____

_____

_____

_____

_____

_____

_____

Week Seven
Cross

Welcome

What has been the heart of your week?

Wonderings

* *Tell about a time you had to give up something good to keep hold of something else that was also good.*
* *I wonder what it's like to feel you're without everything.*
* *I wonder what it's like when a close community breaks apart.*
* *Tell about when there was something you thought you could rely on – and then you couldn't.*

Talk Introduction

Different people find different weeks of this course challenging. For some, the week looking at church and community brings up painful memories. For some, the session two weeks ahead where we look at suffering is a challenge. This week, however, can feel discombobulating for those who have grown up with a different teaching about what Jesus was doing when he died. If you are exploring

Christianity for the first time in this course, then be aware that there may be others in your group who find that this week's teaching raises questions.

Traditionally, churches teach that Jesus died to do something to fix us. This may be to save us from our sins, to conquer the devil or to teach humanity how to live in the face of oppression. Here we learn something different. This week's talk is more of a linear argument but don't worry if you don't get every line. We hope the whole course has been showing you this message: God's only aim is to be with us in Jesus.

Here are two terms that may be new to you:

Easter – the day Jesus rose from the dead.
Ascension – when Jesus went back to be with God in heaven.

Talk: Cross

If there's one word that sums up Jesus' story, that word is *with*. Jesus' ministry, above all else, is about being *with* us, in pain and wonder, in sorrow and in joy, in quiet and in conflict, in death and in life. The Father, the Son and the Holy Spirit are so *with* one another that it seems they are *in* one another. And to the extent that they are *in* one another, we call God not three but one. God is the perfect equilibrium of three persons so *with* that they are *in*, but *in* in such a way that they are still *with*.

Abandonment

Good Friday is the day we see the very heart of God and the very worst in ourselves. Jesus' last words are, 'My God, my God, why have you forsaken me?' At first sight, this is simply the last in a chain of abandonments. Jesus' companions flee, Peter denies, Judas betrays, now God the Father forsakes. It's a litany of desertion. The events leading up to Jesus' crucifixion are a heartless and wholesale disman- tling of *with*. Jesus is left *without* all

> Jesus is still *with* us, but we, at this most precious moment of all, are not *with* him.

those he worked so hard to be *with* – the disciples, the authorities, the poor – and all of them have not just disappeared, but actively deserted or betrayed him. Jesus is still *with* us, but we, at this most precious moment of all, are not *with* him.

But these abandonments are nothing compared to the one that really matters. The cross is a unique event. It's not unique because of how much pain Jesus felt or how much love he'd previously expended. It's unique because the Holy Trinity is the utter presence of unalloyed *with*, and at the moment of Jesus' death, that *with* is, for a brief moment and for the only instant in eternal history, lost.

With is the very essence of God's being within the life of the Trinity (the relationship of God the Father, Son and Holy Spirit), and the very essence of God's being towards us in Christ. And yet at this unique moment, that *with* is obscured. Like the clouds com- ing across the sun, shrouding the earth in shadow, the essence of God, always three persons in perfect relationship, always God's life shaped to be *with* us – that essence is for a moment lost. This is the most poignant and terrifying moment in all history. The two things we think we can know for certain – that God is a Trinity of persons in perfect and eternal relationship and that God is always present *with* us in Christ through the Spirit – these two certainties are, for a moment, taken away. The universe's deepest realities have become unhinged. The Son is not *with* the Father, even though he desper- ately wants to be. The Father is not *with* the Son, breaking our whole notion of their eternal presence one with another. This is the most vivid picture of hell we could imagine: not just our being separated from God, but God being separated from God, God being out of God's own reach.

The cross is Jesus' ultimate demonstration of being *with* us – but in the cruellest irony of all time, it's the instant Jesus finds that neither we, nor the Father, are *with* him. Every aspect of being *not-with*, of being *with-out*, clusters together at this agonizing moment. Jesus experiences the reality of human sin because sin is fundamentally living *without* God. Jesus experiences the depth of suffering because suffering is more than anything the condition of being *without* comfort. Jesus experiences the horror of death because death is the word we give to being *without* all things – without breath, without connectedness, without consciousness, without a body. Jesus experiences the biggest alienation of all, the state of being *without* the Father, and thus being not-God – being, for this moment, without the *with* that is the essence of God.

> Jesus experiences the horror of death because death is the word we give to being *without* all things – without breath, without connectedness, without consciousness, without a body.

And Jesus' words at this most terrifying moment are these: 'My God, my God, why have you forsaken me?' He's still talking to the Father, even at the moment of declaring that the *with* has gone. He's still talking in intimate terms – calling the Father 'My God.' These words come out of the most profound level of trust, the most fathomless depth of *with* and *in*. The most tantalizing thing is that Jesus' last words are a question – a question that doesn't receive an answer. The question should rattle us to our bones.

The question shows us that Jesus has given everything that he is for the cause of being *with* us, for the cause of embracing us within the essence of God's being. He's given so much – even despite our determination to be *without* him. And yet he's given beyond our imagination because for the sake of our being *with* the Father he has, for this moment, lost his own being *with* the Father. And the Father has longed so much to be *with* us that he has, for this moment, lost his being *with* the Son, which is the essence of his being.

Being with us

Here we are, at the central moment in history. Jesus, the incarnate Son of God, has to choose between being with the Father or being with us. And he chooses us. At the same time the Father has to choose between letting the Son be with us or keeping the Son to himself. And he chooses to let the Son be with us. Can you believe it? That is the choice on which our eternal destiny depends. That's the epicentre of the Christian faith, and our very definition of love.

These two astonishing discoveries, the Father's losing the Son for us and the Son's losing the Father for us, rattle our bones because they make us wonder, 'Is all then lost?' – not just for us, but even for God. Has the Trinity lost its identity for nothing? If we don't experience a shiver of this greatest of all horrors at this point, then we haven't allowed ourselves truly to enter Good Friday. But this deepest of fears is what will find an answer two days later, when we find that neither sin nor suffering nor death nor alienation has the last word. *With* is restored at Easter and, on the day of Ascension, *with* has the last word.

> Has the Trinity lost its identity for nothing? If we don't experience a shiver of this greatest of all horrors at this point, then we haven't allowed ourselves truly to enter Good Friday.

Is our alienation from God really so profound that it pushes God to such lengths to reverse and heal it? We don't want to believe it. But here it is, in front of our eyes. That's what the cross is – our cowardice and cruelty confronted by God's wondrous love. Is being *with* us for ever really worth God going to such lengths to secure? Now that is, perhaps, the most awesome question of all. It takes us to the heart of God's identity and the heart of our own. Can we really believe God thought we were worth it? Are our paltry lives worth the Trinity setting aside the essence of its identity in order that we might be *with* God and incorporated into God's life for ever?

Jesus' cry is one of agony that to reach us he had, for a moment, to let go of his Father. What is our cry? Our cry is one of grief that we were not *with* him. It's a cry of astonishment that he was, despite everything, still *with* us. And it's a cry of conviction and commitment that we will be *with* him henceforth and for evermore.

Response

What is your response to this week? Here is some space to note things you don't want to forget and any reflections or questions you would like to take to next week's session.

_____

_____

_____

_____

_____

_____

_____

Week Eight
Prayer

Welcome

What was the heart of your week?

Wonderings

- *Tell about a way you're rich.*
- *Tell about a way you're poor.*
- *I wonder what most amazes you.*
- *I wonder what it's like to feel part of a whole bigger reality.*

Talk Introduction

Whether you are new to exploring faith or have been doing it all your life, prayer can feel intimidating. There may be time in the reflection part of this week's session to raise any general concerns you have or ask about other methods people use to pray. However, we believe prayer is more about the heart than the how, so our talk this week focuses on what we might think as we start to talk to God. It shifts our thinking from prayer being like a vending machine – put in enough coins and you're guaranteed your can of cola – and helps us to think more relationally about those we pray for and about God. We don't approach God as an unknown Santa Claus but we take time to imagine God's thoughts. Next week we look at how to pray for someone who is suffering. But we start by understanding how to be with people as we pray, and how to be with God.

Talk: Prayer

Here are four parts of a conversation you might have with someone from a different place in society from yourself:

- Tell me about the ways you are rich.
- Tell me about the ways you are poor.
- Let me tell you about the ways I am poor.
- Let me tell you about the ways I am rich.

Maybe the conversation might go something like this. You'd say, 'Tell me about the ways you are rich.' And your friend might say, 'I appreciate the way you see me for what I am and not just for what I'm not. My childhood was difficult, but I feel rich in the variety of people my parents brought into my life. My education wasn't very successful but I feel rich in the way I learnt to read people and look into their hearts. I feel rich in the wonder of the birds and their song, the dawn and its beauty, the pouring rain and its refreshment. I've never had much money, but I have a wealth of friends and somehow there's always been someone who's stepped out of the shadows to help me when I couldn't manage everything myself.'

'I appreciate the way you see me for what I am and not just for what I'm not.

And then maybe you'd say, 'Tell me about the ways you are poor.'

And your friend might say, 'You're probably expecting me to talk about how I can't pay the rent and can't find a job. But the real way I feel poor is when I see a person who's a lot worse off than me and I feel powerless to help them. The real times I feel poor are when I see a newcomer to this country trying to make their way and I can't speak enough of their language to be much use to them. The real times I feel poor are when I think of my daughter who died when she was just two and I was just 19, and I miss her with more sadness than I have in my whole heart.'

> 'The real way I feel poor is when I see a person who's a lot worse off than me and I feel powerless to help them.'

And then maybe you'd say, 'May I tell you about the ways I am poor?' And your friend might say, 'I'd never thought of someone like you as poor.' And you might say, 'I felt I had to apologize for being a girl. All my life I've struggled with envy. I've always hated my brother, even though I've never told him and anyone would think we were the best of friends. I wonder if I've ever trusted anyone enough to show them who I really am. 'But I'm also rich. I've always had the ability to concentrate. I can listen, read or even be silent and pray, for hours. And I can paint. I can paint a watercolour, I can paint a miniature, I can paint a wall, I can paint a face, I can paint anything and make it laugh and dance and spring to life. I share my heart through my paintbrush.'

When the two of you have shared your wealth and your poverty with one another in this way, you may want to leave it there. But you may choose to go a little further.

Your friend may say to you, 'Let me tell you about the ways you're rich. You're rich because you don't have to spend every waking moment of your day earning money so you've got time to do beautiful things and walk with people who're in trouble. And let me

'You're poor because you don't have enough people like me around you to tell you the truth about yourself.'

tell you about the ways you're poor. You're poor because you've never found a way to love your brother. You're poor because you don't have enough people like me around you to tell you the truth about yourself.'

And then, ever so tentatively, you may find the courage to say to your friend, 'You're rich because your laugh is infectious and exciting. You're rich because every child you ever meet loves you. You're rich because you've already been through the worst that life can bring so you live without fear. But you're also poor. You're poor because you're deeply hungry to do something really useful for others but you can't find a way to do it.'

'You're rich because every child you ever meet loves you.'

If you have the first kind of interaction, that's called a conversation. But if you have the second kind of interaction, where you talk about each other, that's more than a conversation. That's called a real relationship.

Poverty is a mask we put on a person to cover up their real wealth. And wealth is a disguise we put on a person to hide their profound poverty. Those we call the rich are those in whom we choose to see the wealth but are more reluctant to see the deep poverty. Those we call the poor are those in whom we choose to see the hunger but are slower to see the profound riches. God takes what in each of us is rich and sees through it to our poverty. And God takes our poverty and sees past it to our deeper riches.

Prayer

And every day we enact these words before God. We think of our neighbour, in person, society and globally, and we think about their wealth – and we think of the wonder of God's universe. And we call that praise. We think of our neighbour in their poverty and all that's wrong in the world, and we call that intercession. We think of ourselves in our poverty and of everything we could have done differently, and we call that confession. We think of ourselves in our riches and all the blessings of our life, and we call that

> These are the four parts of prayer: praise, intercession, confession, thanksgiving.

thanksgiving. These are the four parts of prayer: praise, intercession, confession, thanksgiving. The riches of the world, the poverty of the world, the poverty of ourselves, the riches of ourselves. These are the ways we make that courageous intimate conversation a daily act of renewal.

Have that conversation with someone this week. Make it the time you remember that Christ left his wealth and took on your poverty that he might make you wealthy in the way he is wealthy. Make it the time you discover another's poverty and another's wealth, and redefine your own wealth and your own poverty. Have that sacred conversation with another person this week.

But have that conversation with God every day. For that's what prayer is. Prayer is when we see God's wealth and God's poverty, and bring to God our poverty and wealth, and our neighbour's too. That's a daily conversation, in which our friendships, our lives and our world are being transformed.

Response

What is your response to this week? Here is some space to note things you don't want to forget and any reflections or questions you would like to take to next week's session.

_____

_____

_____

_____

_____

_____

Week Nine
Suffering

Welcome

What has been the heart of your week?

Wonderings

- *Tell about a difficult time that proved to be a learning or growing time.*
- *Tell about something helpful someone said to you in a challenging situation.*
- *I wonder what you would say to someone whose closest relative had just been diagnosed with Alzheimer's.*
- *I wonder if you've ever prayed for something and not got it.*

Talk Introduction

How do you respond when someone asks for your prayers or you feel you should say a prayer for someone? This week's talk starts with this question but quickly moves to helping us look at how we respond to people's suffering. How do we respond to our own suffering? The most common way to pray is for the circumstance to be fixed and all to be well. But this isn't the only way. What we learn in this week's talk is that there are other ways for God to be involved in our lives. Sometimes we do see miraculous turnarounds but there are other miracles to be seen. This talk ends looking at how God can transform not just our circumstances, but us.

Talk: Suffering

Let's imagine a conversation over coffee after church. You say hi, you say we haven't talked for a while, you say how are you, what's up, and you catch up on this or that. And then just as you're finishing, your conversation partner holds your forearm, her tone changes and is more serious, and she says, 'Say a prayer for my dad, will you, he's not himself, the dementia's really kicking in now, and I feel like he's losing his identity inch by unrelenting inch.' And you look into your friend's eyes, and in them you see the cost of what it's required to keep going and of what it's taken just to put that pain into words, and you say, 'I'm sorry. I'm so sorry. This must be such a bewildering time for you. Of course I'll pray for your dad. And I'll pray for you too.'

But then you've made a promise, a promise you have to keep. How exactly do you pray for a person in such a situation? What words can you find to wrap around this kind of long, slow-burning tragedy, in which lives and souls unravel and there's no sign of the dawn?

How exactly do you pray for a person in such a situation?

There are two conventional ways to pray for your friend and her dad:

The prayer of resurrection

The first way of praying is a call for a miracle. You just say,

'God, by the power with which you raised Jesus from the dead, restore this man in mind and body, make him himself again, and bring my friend the joy of companionship and the hope of a long and fruitful family life together.'

There's a big part of you that wants to pray this prayer. You love your friend. You see how watching her dad disintegrate before her eyes is breaking her heart. You want God to show some compassion, some change, some action. In the back of your head you maybe have a sense of some other Christians, perhaps close to you, who seem to pray for resurrection all the time, and you wonder if you should have more faith and expect God to do amazing things every day. But you've also seen hopes dashed, you've seen Alzheimer's only end one way, and a part of you can't even say the word 'heal' because it seems to be asking for something that just isn't going to happen. That's the prayer of resurrection. You know Christianity's founded on it and you know it's what your friend most longs for – but sometimes you just find it too hard to say.

But that's not the only kind of prayer.

The prayer of incarnation

The second conventional kind of prayer is a call for the Holy Spirit to be with your friend and her father. It's a recognition that Jesus was broken, desolate, alone, on the brink of death, and that this is all part of being a human being, all part of the deal you sign on to the day you're born. Our bodies and minds are fragile, frail and sometimes feeble. There's no guarantee life will be easy, comfortable, fun or happy. The prayer of incarnation says:

'God, in Jesus you shared our pain, our foolishness and our sheer bad luck; you took on our flesh with all its needs and clumsiness and weakness. Visit my friend and her father now: give them patience to endure what lies ahead, hope to get through every trying day and companions to show them your love.'

The irony about this prayer is that the resurrection prayer expects God to do all the work, whereas this prayer stirs us into action ourselves. If we say, 'Send them companions to show them your love', we've got to be wondering if there's anyone better placed to be such a companion than we ourselves. Deep down your friend is well aware that the prospects for her father are pretty bleak. What she's really asking for when she nervously puts her hand out to clasp your forearm is, 'Help me trust that I'm not alone in all of this.' Chances are, you can help her with that. But in the midst of it all you'd hardly be human if you didn't feel powerless and inadequate in the face of all she was going through.

> 'Help me trust that I'm not alone in all of this.'

The prayer of transfiguration

I want to suggest that resurrection and incarnation aren't the only kinds of prayer. I'm sure they're the most common, and in many circumstances they say pretty much all we want, need or ought to say. But there's a third kind of prayer – the prayer of transfiguration:

'God, in your son's transfiguration we see a whole reality within, beneath and beyond what we thought we understood; in their times of bewilderment and confusion, show my friend and her father your glory, that they may find a deeper truth to their life than they ever knew, make firmer friends than they ever had, discover reasons for living beyond what they'd ever imagined, and be folded into your grace like never before.'

This is a different kind of a prayer. The prayer of resurrection has a certain defiance about it – in the face of what seem to be all the known facts, it calls on God to produce the goods and turn the situation around. It has courage and hope but there's always that fear that it has a bit of fantasy as well. The prayer of incarnation is honest and unflinching about the present and the future, but you could say it's a little too much swathed in tragedy.

Maybe this is your real prayer for your friend and her father. Maybe this is your real prayer for yourself, in the midst of whatever it is you're wrestling with today. Not so much, 'Fix this and take it off my desk!' nor even, 'Be with me and share in my struggle, now and always' but something more like:

'Make this trial and tragedy, this problem and pain, a glimpse of your glory, a window into your world, when I can see your face, sense the mystery in all things and walk with angels and saints. Bring me closer to you in this crisis than I ever have been in calmer times. Make this a moment of truth, and when I cower in fear and feel alone, touch me, raise me and make me alive like never before.'

Response

What is your response to this week? Here is some space to note things you don't want to forget and any reflections or questions you would like to take to next week's session.

_____

_____

_____

_____

_____

_____

_____

Week Ten
Resurrection

Welcome

What has been the heart of your week?

Wonderings

- *Tell about a truly wonderful day.*
- *Tell about a day when something that had seemed a burden was turned into a gift.*
- *I wonder, if you could change one thing about the world, what it would be.*
- *I wonder if you have one possession that somehow contains or represents a lot of other possessions.*

Talk Introduction

This is a week to reflect. What are you taking with you as you end this time with this group? What have you become that you don't want to lose? This week's talk reflects over the whole of human history leading us to the day that creates the possibility of endless days.

Talk: Resurrection

Imagine you're in heaven and you're looking back on eternity to select the very best day of them all. We could suggest six finalists and consider their merits. Let's take them in chronological order:

How about the day of creation?

This day has fabulous fireworks. It's got exponential imagination. It's the day the inner imagination of God got externalized and turned into tangible form. Do you think the whole history of the universe was contained in embryo on this day, like a tiny egg that contains a person's whole future?

Our second candidate is the day of the exodus

This is the great day when God parted the Red Sea and took the descendants of Abraham, who'd been enslaved in Egypt, to freedom. Everyone was awestruck by the power and purpose of God. Just imagine the collective joy and discovery that nothing was impossible with God. Great day.

Our third candidate is the day of the covenant

On this day God gave Moses the Ten Commandments and God's commitment to Moses' people crystallized in promises, guarantees and tangible forms of loyalty and love. It was the day that defined what it meant to be God's people and how to live for ever in peace with God and one another. It was the original mountain-top experience.

Then to our fourth candidate: it's Christmas

This is the day we discover that God loved us so much as to become one like us. God affirmed creation so deeply that, despite our sin, God thought it was worth entering our life, taking on our mantle and inhabiting our existence. God coming at Christmas was the reason for creation. God made the world in order to be with us in Christ.

But then there's Good Friday

On the day of the exodus God's people saw God's power. On Good Friday we see God's love. Hands that flung stars into space to cruel nails surrendered. What wondrous love. Could any day surpass this?

Well, here's a candidate: what about the Last Day?

The last day of all. The day when Christ comes back. The day when everything that's been wrong in all the history of time gets set right, when all who've been downtrodden are seated on thrones, and all who've lost their lives in tragedy find untold joy. The day when evil is finally expunged and sin can plague us no more. The day when everything that creation was meant to be but never quite became is transformed and creation is restored, iridescent, changed from glory into glory and showered in wonder, love and praise. Beat that.

Well, I think we can beat the Last Day.

The Day of Days

Early in the morning, depending on which version of the story you read, there was one woman, or three, or two men, who went to a tomb. It's a day that began as one of the saddest-ever days. But before breakfast time it had turned into the *Day of Days* – not just the greatest day of them all, but the day that contained all the other six. Just see how this day, this holiest, most astonishing and wondrous day, is all the other six days wrapped into one.

It's another *Creation Day* because look, it's Jesus and Mary, a man and a woman in a garden, just like creation, and it's a day of limitless possibility. It's almost literally the first day – the first day of Christianity, of the past released by forgiveness and the future unleashed by eternal life. It's the beginning of everything. It's the Great Day.

And look, it's another *exodus*. Moses and his people were led out of the slavery of the Egyptians – we this day are set free from evil, sin and death. It's the exodus again, but not just for a small number of people long ago; this time it's for everyone, for ever. It's the end of the night of suffering and misery and the dawn of the eternal day of glory, hope and joy.

And see how it's another *Covenant*. The first covenant came with smoke, earthquake and fire. This one too came with portents surrounding Christ's death and an earthquake that moved the stone. The first covenant showed Israel how to stay close to God; this one shows everyone that nothing can separate us from the love of God – not even death itself. Whatever we throw at God, however deeply we reject God, however much we seek to bury or destroy God, God will find a way back to us. That's the truest covenant of all.

> Whatever we throw at God, however deeply we reject God, however much we seek to bury or destroy God, God will find a way back to us.

60

And look how it's like *Christmas* all over again, but bigger. Christmas affirms the fleshly, tangible, earthiness of human existence. Easter does so again, but this time after humanity has demonstrated one almighty allergic reaction to the goodness of God. Everything the incarnation proclaims and embodies, the resurrection affirms twice over: God will be with us in Christ, not just out of primordial purpose, but even when we have done our absolute darnedest to expunge Christ from our presence. Resurrected life is bodily. The human body has an eternal destiny.

And most obviously, Easter is *Good Friday* again. Jesus shows his disciples his hands and his side. He is the good shepherd who has laid down his life for his sheep. And now on this blessed morning he begins to go around reassembling his flock, starting with Mary Magdalene. Good Friday shows us that God will be with us even if it splits God's heart in two, even if it threatens to sever the inner-Trinitarian relationship of the Father and the Son. Easter shows us that nothing whatsoever can stop God being with us, not just at the most intense moment in history – but for ever.

And then finally Easter is everything the *Last Day* will be, but in microcosm. Like the Last Day, Easter restores creation. Like the Last Day, Easter vindicates the oppressed – in this case Jesus – and exalts the humble and meek. Like the Last Day, Easter is the enactment of every single one of the Beatitudes. Jesus is the pure in heart. Jesus is the peacemaker. Jesus is the one who hungers and thirsts for righteousness. Jesus is the one who is reviled by all people. And on the day of resurrection he's happy, he's blessed, he's called God's child, he's laughing.

This *Day of Days*, this wondrous, glorious, blessed, fabulous day – this day is the greatest day in the history of the universe and the story of heaven. This is the perfect seventh day, the day that comprises, epitomizes, embodies and expresses all the other six great days of all time. This is the day on which all the suffering, all the imagination, all the love, all the freedom, all the grief, all the justice, all the hope, all the wonder are combined in a mixing bowl, left behind a huge stone, and like yeast acting on a mixture, burst out, push that stone away because there's so much life there nothing can keep it in, no one can keep it down, no force in heaven or earth can stop it now.

This is the day. This is the great day. This is the glorious day. This is creation, liberation, incarnation and consummation all wrapped into one. This is the day when we stand on the shoulders of God and say, 'I can see for ever!' This is Easter Day.

Response

What is your response to this week? Here is some space to note things you don't want to forget.

_____

_____

_____

_____

_____

_____

_____